Dedication

This Almanac is dedicated to my love, Garnett Strother,
who always reminds me that mindset is everything.

Who uplifts and inspires me.

Who sees my potential and will not let me be anything less.

I would not be who I am without him in my life.

I adore you always. xoxox

Gala Darling

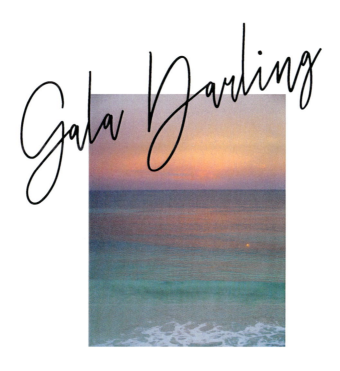

2018 EDITION

RADICAL SELF-LOVE ALMANAC

CONTENTS

2018

MONTHS

11 *January*	54 *July*
24 *February*	64 *August*
30 *March*	70 *September*
36 *April*	78 *October*
42 *May*	85 *November*
47 *June*	89 *December*

FOR BEST USE

Keep this Almanac beside your bed for easy reference. Fill out the activity sheets with a hot pink Sharpie. Take photos of the pages that mean the most to you and keep them on your phone. Take every day as it comes. Make feeling good your first priority. Remember that self-love is never selfish.

INTRODUCTION

Welcome to our 2018 Almanac! This is our third year running, and this edition is on a whole new level because it's in print! I can't tell you how excited I am for you to be able to hold this in your hands and carry it with you. My hope is that it fills you with inspiration and becomes a friendly companion as you journey through your year.

Let's not beat around the bush: 2017 was rough. Many of my favourite moments were when I was out of the USA, in Morocco, or Mexico, or Indonesia, far away from the craziness. Coming back to New York City was hard every single time, but it did inspire some desperately-needed changes in my life. I started to change my social media habits, and limited myself to floundering around in the internet depths for only a couple of hours a day. Instead of endlessly scrolling through Twitter and Instagram in moments of boredom—and inevitably being faced with some new horror—I would read, instead. Or write. Or meditate. Or go for a walk. Or call a friend. The benefits of this new routine were twofold: I inoculated myself against the terror that seemed to be flung at everyone on a daily basis, which made me more peaceful, less panicked, and less reactionary. And it also increased my creativity and productivity. It gave me the opportunity to dive deep into my mind and make new things that really excited me. I cannot overstate how beautiful it was to regain my sense of focus, instead of working for 45 seconds and then flipping to another tab.

When life is crazy—and no doubt, it is—it is up to us to create systems to help us cope, bring us peace, and—crucially—enhance our world. Being in survival mode is not enough. We want to thrive, to fill our lives with magic and adventure, to love wildly and without fear. Fear and hysteria is being thrown at us at a rate that we have never experienced before as a species, and it is our responsibility to say when enough is enough, and to step off the treadmill. Our brains are simply not made to process so much trauma, and so we have to protect ourselves. For me, limiting social media access and recommitting to feeling joy was absolutely imperative.

I want to encourage you to truly take care of yourself this year.

To step into radical self love on a daily basis. This is not a selfish act: radical self love is also about taking care of those around you. Be generous, share your resources, give your time, practice empathy, and be kind. We need each other more than ever. Throw yourself into your community, hold your friends close, and indulge in pleasure as much as you can. Don't let uncertainty suffocate you and the gifts you have to share.

And don't worry: there are plenty of ideas on exactly how you can do this throughout this Almanac. I'd love to hear how you integrate them into your life! You can always email me at **love@galadarling.com** or just tag me on Instagram (**@galadarling**). Hearing from you makes my day, so don't be shy! ♥

Gala xx

The Empress

The card I've pulled for us for 2018 is The Empress, and I cannot tell you how happy this makes me! What a beautiful card. To me, the Empress is the queen of the entire deck. She is the embodiment of powerful femininity, the Divine Mother, the baddest bitch. The Empress surveys her land and knows every peak and valley. She is creative and abundant, her imagination helping to provide her with all the physical wealth she desires. She is in full possession of her skills and uses them wisely, bringing them to fruition in the world. For those of you who dream of having children, the Empress also signifies fertility.

Pulling this card simply reinforces my belief that 2018 is about women rising to their powerful potential, taking leadership roles, and redefining how our lives look. We will no longer take a back seat, accept crumbs, or feel comfortable being second-class citizens. As CREATORS OF THE WORLD, as givers of life, as the primary creative force on this planet, we have officially had enough of the bullshit. We are starting our own revolution, and it is inclusive, it is intersectional, it is unshakeable.

HOW TO BRING THE EMPRESS INTO YOUR YEAR

- **Be alone enough that you know your own thoughts.** So many of us are overly influenced by what we see or read elsewhere, and we're not totally sure of our own opinions. This year, make sure to get in touch with your inner truth. Get clear on your own dreams, desires, ethics, and morals.

- **And then... Speak your truth, even—and especially—when it feels difficult, uncomfortable, or unwelcome.** This will get easier with time, but it requires a little persistence and courage. By the way, it's okay to excuse yourself from places where it is clear your opinion is not being heard. It's not your job to educate everyone around you.

- **Spend time with your creative impulses.** Think about the things that you wished existed, and get busy making them! Go deep, bury yourself in your creative conquests. Turn your phone off and see how that changes the scope of your imagination. There is no limit to this, only your imagination!

- **Reconnect with your body.** It's not just a bag of flesh that carries you from here to there: your body is a holy place, your own unique temple, and there are neverending secrets and discoveries contained within it. Connecting with your body could be dance class, tantra, learning to be present during sex, intimacy coaching, exercise, yoga… The list goes on. A lot of us ignore our bodies and focus primarily on our minds, but we are missing such an enormous piece of our own divinity when we do.

- **Cultivate a spiritual practice.** This could be anything—meditation, tapping, prayer, weekly sound healings… Whatever floats your boat. But it is essential to have something that is for you and you alone, a time to clear your mind and be with yourself. It's the best antidepressant on the planet. Deeper in the Almanac, you'll find a piece on how to create a Sacred Morning practice! Go find it!

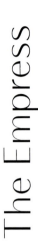

The Empress

- **Support other women.** Truly standing in your power as the Empress means you are not threatened by other women and you refuse to buy into the bullshit paradigm that we are all competing with another. This belief is driven by the patriarchy and it keeps us separate. Imagine what we could do if we REFUSED to compete, and instead, banded together! We would crush every oppressor in our wake. Learn to see yourself as a beautiful, unique genius… And other women as the same. Trust me: no one comes close to you. This fear will only hold you back, keep you small, and fuck up your shit. Don't fall for it.

Let us join together and embrace the Empress within every single one of us… And let us use the Empress as our guide, as our goddess, in the year of 2018. ❤

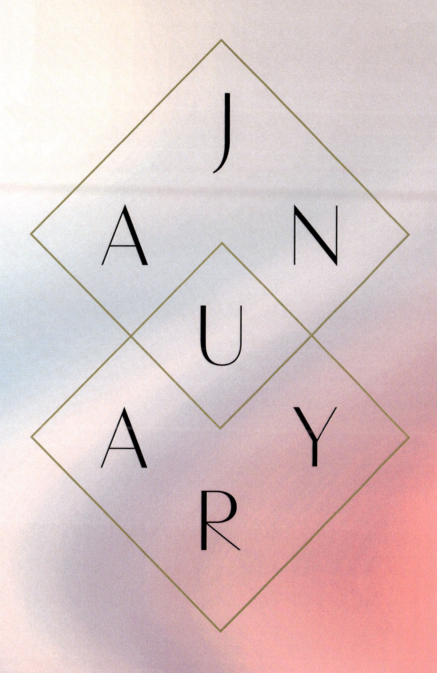

"YOU HAVE TO ACT AS IF IT WERE POSSIBLE TO RADICALLY TRANSFORM THE WORLD, AND YOU HAVE TO DO IT ALL THE TIME." —ANGELA DAVIS

ACTIVITY SHEET

THE WORD I CHOOSE TO EMBODY IN JANUARY IS:

_____

I am embodying this word when I do the following:

_____
_____
_____

If I ever feel stuck or tripped up, I will think of these people to re-inspire me:

_____
_____
_____

MY BIGGEST GOAL FOR JANUARY IS:

_____

In order to make my dream real, I need to start with the following:

_____
_____
_____
_____
_____

YOUR MAGICAL

xoxoxoxo

YEAR

This is not your normal goal-setting! No!

We are not going to write an enormous list of insurmountable tasks and then try to work up the desire to tick them off. That is not fun and it does not feel good. In the words of Abraham-Hicks, "All is well, and you will never get it done." Let's stop pretending like our to-do lists will ever really be finished. Instead, we should choose to focus our attention on things that make us feel good, and take it from there.

In that spirit, we are going to take a moment to consider how we want to *feel* and then use *that* information to set our targets for 2018.

Using your emotions as a guiding light for goal-setting is something I learned from the incomparable Danielle LaPorte. She has a wonderful book all about the subject called *The Desire Map* that you should absolutely pick up. Essentially, her argument is that if the way you want to feel is out of alignment with your goals, even if you hit every single target, you'll feel like crap. And of course, this is true! If your biggest desire is to feel freedom, then opening a retail store which requires you to be in one place six days out of the week is going to feel dismal, even if the business is doing well.

The idea is to come up with a handful of words that demonstrate how you want to feel. Maybe "radiant, free, open". Or "excited, powerful, connected". It's up to you. Brainstorm on it, and take your time!

Danielle also recommends writing your Core Desired Feelings (your CDFs, if you will) at the top of your planner, or on a sticky note on your desk, or anywhere you will see them regularly. Having these available to glance at will help guide your decision-making as you move throughout the year.

Another thing I recommend doing is Tony Robbins' test to see which of the six essential human needs most drives you at core.tonyrobbins.com/driving-force. By answering ten simple questions, you will discover which of your needs is most important, and how that can be either an asset or a downfall. If you write your primary need into your planner, you can remind yourself of what you really need to feel satisfied in life. You may find that you're not bored or miserable—you're just not meeting your primary need often enough! ♥

ACTIVITY SHEET

My Core Desired Feelings are:

_____
_____
_____
_____
_____
_____
_____
_____
_____
_____
_____
_____
_____

My goals for 2018 are:

_____
_____
_____
_____
_____
_____
_____
_____
_____
_____
_____
_____
_____

2020

Sturdy 07

THINGS TO DO IN WINTER

WINTER LIST

1. Come up with the perfect hot chocolate recipe (Nutella hot chocolate is my all-time favourite)
2. Pledge to wear bright lipstick every single day
3. Invest in a massaging seat cushion that heats up (it will change your life)
4. Get a Vitamin B12 shot (or buy a vitamin vape pen!)
5. Buy a pink or purple sheepskin (or faux) rug to put beside your bed
6. Use doTerra On Guard oil (or throat drops) to keep your immune system strong
7. Say "I love you" in the mirror every morning
8. Write fortune cookie-sized affirmations and put them in all the pockets of your clothing and handbags
9. Slather yourself in deliciously-scented oil every night before bed
10. Listen to as many episodes of RuPaul's podcast as you can
11. Watch all your favourite childhood movies
12. Make a playlist for your favourite person and plan a cozy night in to listen to it together
13. Install coloured or LED light bulbs all over your house
14. Get a pedicure, strictly for your own pleasure
15. Buy yourself a sparkly glass and keep it on your desk so you remember to stay hydrated
16. Watch every episode of 30 Rock
17. Embrace the holiday spirit by really helping someone else who needs it
18. Hang photos of you and your best friends all over your house
19. Lie in sunspots as much as you can
20. Kiss someone with your whole body

Let us not beat around the bush, my friends. The most important thing in life is to feel good. If you don't feel good, you will drag your shitty feelings behind you like a deflated parachute that picks up every crumb, piece of lint, and stray dog poop. One of the most effective ways to cut that parachute loose is to actively work on raising your vibration in the morning.

That is why, today, I want to talk to you about the concept of Sacred Mornings.

A lot of us act as if we don't have enough time to do what we want to do, but that is just an excuse. Anyone—no matter how busy your life is—can find an hour in the morning. Brian Tracy calls this "setting the table", but that's not very sexy, which is why I prefer to think of this as a Sacred Morning practice.

Now, here's the thing you might not be expecting me to say. This idea works best without a lot of structure, rules, or conditions.

Why?

Because when we cover ourselves with rules and conditions, what we are essentially saying is that we cannot be happy unless this condition is met. We do this all the time. "I will be happy when he texts me back. Or I lose 10 pounds. Or I get one more client." Nonsense. Bullshit. Stop that! The greatest lesson we will ever learn is to be happy no matter what. So why not begin as soon as your eyes flutter open? It's only logical.

Imagine how different your day would be if you made the effort to feel joy first thing!

WHAT DOES A SACRED MORNING LOOK LIKE?

Maybe the best part of a Sacred Morning is that you have the opportunity to make your bed your temple. God, how delicious. I like to layer my bed up with cozy pink and grey sheets and then cover it all with a psychedelic bedspread, but it's up to you. Want to surround your bed with crystals (or even glue them onto your headboard)? DO IT! Want a pink faux sheepskin on the floor next to the bed so you squish your toes into something lovely when you finally rise and shine? MAKE IT HAPPEN! Want to layer your bedding with a scrumptious throw? WHAT THE FUCK ARE YOU WAITIN' FOR?!

NOW THAT YOU'VE SET THE SCENE, HERE'S HOW IT WORKS.

A Sacred Morning is one that feels good. When we go to sleep, all the momentum from the previous day—which, ideally, was a day where we focussed on what we want, appreciated what we already have, and lived firmly and delightfully in the present—dissipates. So when we wake up, we need to get back on that train: the train of joy and excitement.

The goal of a Sacred Morning is to juice yourself up and raise your vibration. The only rules are that a) it has to feel good, and b) it should be focussed on you (and not on

Maybe the best part of a Sacred Morning is that you have the opportunity to make your bed your temple. God, how delicious.

other people). This means that scrolling through Instagram looking at other people's lives first thing in the morning is not part of the practice!

My mornings are different every time... Because fuck the rules, and fuck the conditions! What feels good this morning will feel like a drag tomorrow. Give yourself the gift of flexibility, exercise your spontaneity muscles, test out your intuition. Free yourself up.

WANT IDEAS? YOU MIGHT LIKE TO TRY...

• **MEDITATING!** You could just close your eyes for five minutes and visualise all the things you're thankful for. You could do the Creation Space meditation with Danielle LaPorte. You could chill with Abraham Hicks, or Louise Hay, or blow your mind with Jessica Snow. You could queue up some rain or ocean sounds and bliss out. There are so many ways to make this feel great, and it is such a beautiful way to bring yourself into alignment with yourself.

• **SINGING!** Put on your favourite album and raise your voice. Chant along to something that makes you feel empowered and sparkly.

• **WORKING OUT!** The entire Bad Witch Workout Starter Pack (badwitchworkout.org) can be done in your living room, no equipment required (and I promise you'll feel absolutely amazing afterwards). Go to a Pilates class. Jump up and down. Dance like a wild thing. The great thing about moving first thing in the morning is that it throws your energy level up to a thousand, and keeps your mood elevated all day long. Who doesn't want that?!

• **STRETCH!** Do bed yoga with Tara Stiles, or unroll a yoga mat in your living room and crawl onto it to stretch out all your tight muscles. You could watch Yogaglo or just do what feels good in the moment.

• **JOURNALLING!** You don't have to use a pen and paper if that feels arduous. Go for the path of least resistance! I type all my thoughts because it's so much faster and I can get more down in a shorter amount of time. Remove all the obstacles that stop you from wanting to do this, because it's a fantastic way of processing your feelings, clearing out stale emotions, and working through the things in your life.

• **GRATITUDE!** My mermaid Alexandra Roxo and I have just started this as part of our morning practice: we make voice memos and text them through to each other. It's so good to get deliberately juicy and share it, and then listen to what's good in her life! You can also write your gratitude, yell it aloud in the shower, tell it to your dog, call your mother and share it, or write it on a note and put it in your beloved's pocket.

• **SELF-PLEASURE!** I mean... I probably don't have to extol the virtues of this practice to you. But I'd like to mention a few things to amp it up. For example... Chakrubs. (I have a rose quartz one, OBVS.) You could add in a yoni egg practice. You could lose yourself in the ecstasy of a Jimmyjane vibrator (the Form 2 is my pick and I cannot be without it). And if you REALLY want to ascend to the next level... Visualise what you want at the moment of orgasm and beam it out into the universe. This is sex magic, and it's rad as shit. MEOW!

Sounds good, right? Get into it! ♥

ADVICE

"Hey Gala, I've realised some girls I adore and have known for years are actually quite bitchy and fundamentally, I don't get on with them. Help!"
—*Gloria*

After making yourself feel good, one of the most important ways we can guard and protect our energy is to ensure that the people we spend time with make us feel good too. Don't write them off straight away; give them the opportunity to be the people you know they can be. Why not tell them that your focus is on feeling good, and talking about other people behind their backs doesn't help you with that mission? See what they say. You might be surprised! But if they don't get it or aren't on board, let it go and trust that people who match your vibration are on their way. In my experience, only people who are chronically unhappy with their lives bitch about other people. You don't need that kind of energy in your life! ❤

10 REASONS WHY IT'S GREAT TO BE AN
Aquarius

1. You're so self-sufficient, you'll never be bored with your own company!

2. You're idealistic to the end: Aquarians really do believe that we are all one and love is everything

3. You're truly free-spirited

4. Creativity is your middle name—you'll never do anything the standard way

5. You own your weirdness without shame

6. You will always stand up for what you believe is right

7. You can give every other sign a run for their money when it comes to eccentricity

8. You're so tech-savvy, and always up on the latest developments

9. As ultimate humanitarians and philanthropists, your heart is always in the right place

10. You can make friends with anyone and communicate easily with a wide range of people

"WHEN YOU CHANGE THE WAY YOU LOOK AT THINGS,
THE THINGS YOU LOOK AT CHANGE." —ESTHER HICKS

ACTIVITY SHEET

THIS MONTH, I WILL PRACTICE RADICAL SELF LOVE BY DOING THE FOLLOWING:

_____
_____
_____
_____
_____
_____

When I am feeling bad about myself, I will remember that I am _____

When I am feeling sad about life, I will remember that _____ exists, _____ is real, and I am looking forward to _____

No matter what happens, I am so grateful for _____

I am always attracting and creating the things I am thinking about, so this month I am going to think about _____ and _____ and definitely _____!

HOW TO CELEBRATE *Valentine's Day*

WITHOUT LOSING YOUR GODDAMN MIND

Valentine's Day was the genesis of the radical self love movement. I had started my own journey to self-love back in 2006, but it all came together—and got a name—on Valentine's Day in 2011.

I remember sitting at my desk, browsing blogs and Twitter, and seeing so much sadness, frustration and overwhelm. I was flummoxed by the way that this nonsense holiday would send so many women into a tizzy. And these weren't basic babes, either— they were badasses. They ran their own companies, wrote their own rules, and wore thigh-high boots to family dinners! They had an inherent sense of their own self-worth… But somehow, on February 14th, that all went out the window. Suddenly, their value was only visible if it was reflected back at them by someone else.

Of course, we know that this doesn't work. But we get confused by how to put it into practice.

THE FIRST RULE OF HAPPINESS IS THAT OTHER PEOPLE HAVE TO BE IRRELEVANT TO IT.

When we make someone else's opinion about us more important than our own, we are walking into a world of misery (and might I add, bullshit). How could anyone else ever know more about you than you? YOU are inside of you all the time. You are the sovereign of your own nation. You know exactly who you are and you know exactly what you want. The only reason why you would ever feel insecure or uncertain about these things is because you are not taking enough time to yourself.

So how can we navigate this insane holiday without completely losing our shit?

The first thing we need to do is become practiced at creating our own world. For example, mine is called the Galaverse. (It's bigger than just a world. It's mammoth.) I work at creating this place all the time: with my Sacred Morning practice, by decorating my home with colours and things that I love, by spraying myself with fragrance that lights me up, by making feeling good a priority, by doing something creative every day, by surrounding myself with people who are fun and inspiring, and so on.

When you are active in this process—of engineering the world that you want to live in—these external circumstances (like Valentine's Day, or whether or not someone sent you flowers) start to become less and less relevant. They don't shake your mood. Plus, you know you can always buy flowers for yourself!

Another thing that you can do if you're feeling bad or sad about Valentine's Day is to simply change the record in your mind. Becoming aware of the thoughts that you think is immensely powerful, because once you realise what you're doing, you have the ability to stop yourself in your tracks! So if you find yourself going into a bummer spiral, you can think something else. Do a gratitude list in your head or even out loud. (I like to recite them aloud when I walk my dog Cleo. I think she thinks hearing them, too.) Or you can take it a step further and use your body to help change your energy. Jump up and down, have an orgasm, take a nap, dance or sing, or call a friend and get out of the house.

Loving, appreciating, forgiving, and repeatedly choosing yourself over and over again is no small feat.

If you already know that Valentine's Day tends to be a hard one for you, organise a social excursion ahead of time. Grab your best friend and go out and have a fabulous day. Maybe a mani/pedi date, a trip to an art gallery, or a killer shopping excursion are exactly what the doctor ordered.

Finally, why not spend Valentine's Day celebrating the love you have for yourself? Loving, appreciating, forgiving, and repeatedly choosing yourself over and over again is no small feat. It takes tremendous strength to continually rise to the occasion, to be your best self, and to never give up on yourself! When you have and do those things, falling in love with someone else is like adding a candle to the top of a birthday cake. It is already deeply splendiferous and glorious. That candle adds something magical, sure—but it is not the be all and end all.

THIS VALENTINE'S DAY… BE YOUR OWN BIRTHDAY CAKE. ♥

ADVICE

"The last 7 years have been all about rebuilding my foundation. I left my crappy husband, got sober, went into therapy for my ED, dealt with a death, went from being insecure to being happy in my own skin. However, I haven't had the motivation to have a consistent practice in what I love (writing, speaking and art). I am no longer depressed and broken, but I feel lost! I thought I would have so much energy/motivation, but I don't. Any ideas?" —*Sara*

Life moves in cycles and yours is no exception. Your last seven years have been the definition of transformative and regenerative, and it takes time to come back to equilibrium after so much change! Give yourself a moment to breathe. The next piece of this journey is about working to create your own world so that you feel lit up and inspired. Inspiration comes from inside, from feeling good in yourself. Motivation is external and it never lasts. Commit to a Sacred Morning practice and see how that reignites your creativity! Every little piece of writing you do will remind you of how good it feels to do it, and then you will feel inspired to do even more of it. Keep building the momentum, and before you know it, you'll be waking up ecstatic every morning. ♥

10 REASONS WHY IT'S GREAT TO BE A
Pisces

1. Always ready to go beneath the surface
2. Not afraid of feelings
3. Your life is your art
4. Pisces truly does care about the people around them
5. Romantic as fuck
6. The ability to see beauty in everything and everyone
7. Intuition on point
8. Your imagination is unparalleled
9. You have the ability to heal yourself and others
10. Your sensitivity makes you extra-perceptive and open to the energy of the universe

MARCH

"IF YOU ARE WILLING TO LOOK AT ANOTHER PERSON'S BEHAVIOR TOWARD YOU AS A REFLECTION OF THE STATE OF THEIR RELATIONSHIP WITH THEMSELVES RATHER THAN A STATEMENT ABOUT YOUR VALUE AS A PERSON, THEN YOU WILL, OVER A PERIOD OF TIME, CEASE TO REACT AT ALL." —YOGI BHAJAN

ACTIVITY SHEET

THIS MONTH, I WILL HONOR MY BODY BY:
_____

The hardest part of doing this is being organised, so I will make my life easier by:
_____
_____
_____

When I look in the mirror and wish I was looking at something different, I will tell myself:
_____
_____
_____

I will remember that I have come such a long way and:
_____
_____
_____

I will blow myself a kiss in the mirror and say:
_____
_____
_____

I will remember that every day is a fresh reset, and I can be the _____ that I know I am!

BEING HAPPY WITHOUT CONDITIONS

You might be surprised to hear this, but being joyful and in a state of radiance is *your natural state*. When you have been feeling depressed, anxious, sad, or full of dread for a long time, it is because you have allowed your environment to derail you from your true self. You have been looking around at the "reality" of your situation—perhaps a soul-sucking job, a shitty relationship, or a bummer living situation—and you have become seduced by its apparent "realness".

This isn't surprising. We are *all* seduced by what we see around us and we are convinced that these are the circumstances of our lives. But the truth is that we are always creating newer, better things in our lives... And part of bringing them into being is in *believing that you can have them right now*.

But we're getting ahead of ourselves. What I really want to talk to you about today is the idea that we place conditions on our happiness all the time.

As humans, we have a tendency to keep joy just out of reach. We're not even conscious that we're doing it. We are walking reactionaries, recoiling from interactions and completely thrown off our game by other people's behaviour. We allow our lovers, parents, friends and workmates to dictate our mood. When they "behave" in a way that we approve of, we feel okay. (Although we can even overthink that—'Why is he/she being so nice? They must be guilty of something!'—sound familiar?) And when they *don't* do what we want them to do, we get mad. Bitter. Resentful. We punish them... But mostly we punish *ourselves*, because as long as we are feeling bad, it is impossible to feel good!

Read that again.

When we are mad, we are punishing ourselves, because as long as we are feeling bad, it is impossible to feel good!

And feeling good is where we are at our best. Feeling good is our natural state. It is where we are supposed to be, and it is where we *will always be* unless we *think ourselves out of it*. Feeling good is where we can dream and create a bigger, brighter future. It's where we get our best ideas and manifest our wildest desires.

Have you ever noticed that when you're feeling bad—angry, or sorry for yourself, or "stuck"—nothing flows? Nothing works. You don't have lightning bolt, life-changing ideas. You don't see the best in your partner. You don't give anyone the benefit of the doubt. Instead, you stay locked into your bad mood, kicking up a little dust cloud of misery everywhere you go. Often, this dust cloud will follow you until you go to sleep. Thankfully, when you go to bed, your momentum gets reset and you can start the day fresh!

When we remove conditions from our joy, we are so empowered. One of the biggest ways to do this is to stop being thrown about by other people's behaviour. In other words, make other people irrelevant to your happiness!

For example, if I see an acquaintance and she isn't as

When we remove conditions from our joy, we are so empowered. One of the biggest ways to do this is to stop being thrown about by other people's behaviour.

---

friendly as I hoped she would be, I can choose not to take it personally. (It's her stuff, after all.) I don't let our interaction kick up a big dust cloud that distracts me from the more important things on my plate: feeling good, being creative, giving love to the people around me. If my man is cranky, I don't take that personally either. (He probably just has low blood sugar. Snacks always help.) I don't have to start an argument or get sucked into his vibe. I always have the choice to go into another room, or go for a walk, or simply step up my own energy... Because one of the coolest things is that when my frequency is turned up really high, *other people cannot help but join me in it*. A big, super-tuned, brightly glowing vibration is irresistible to others. It is *contagious*.

This might sound like a lot. It might also sound like rubbish, and I understand that, because we're talking about some pretty abstract concepts. "Vibration?" Sure! It sounds weird. I get it. But I want to ask you, when is the last time you AMPED UP your good vibes in response to someone else's bad vibes? You might not even be able to recall a time that you did that. So many of us go into automatic reaction or join our friend where they are, and it never works, right? It never makes them feel better, or you feel better. Let's try something different. Next time someone you care about is in a bad mood, remember these words, and crank the imaginary dial on your own frequency. Push it up to 11,

baby! Keep it there. Bring your full joy and appreciation and glee. And see what happens.

The second piece of this puzzle is that *once* you turn up your vibration, you have to stop caring about whether or not the other person joins you there. Because—gasp!—that is a condition you're placing on your happiness! See how that works?

Here's the scenario. Your beloved is in a bad mood. Maybe they're tired, maybe they're hungry, maybe they had a rough day. In a flash of brilliance, you remember this piece and decide not to pick a fight, and not to dull your shine to try to meet them where they are. Instead, you turn up the radiance. Maybe you dance around the living room… Maybe you tell a joke… Maybe you start writing a gratitude list, or ask them to join you in speaking one out loud. BUT—and here's the kicker—you don't take their response personally. You don't *need* them to join you where you are. Your goal is to focus so hard on feeling good that it *doesn't matter* whether they change their mindset or not. Your goal is to keep feeling good for as long as possible.

Give this a try next time it happens. See what occurs. I think you'll be surprised by what transpires. ♥

ADVICE

10 REASONS WHY IT'S GREAT TO BE AN

Aries

1. Firestarter energy

2. You always act on your ideas

3. When you're passionate about something, you will focus on it until you physically cannot anymore

4. Loyal to a fault

5. You always know best!

6. You don't mind being alone if it's what will make you happiest

7. You're absolutely oblivious to peer pressure

8. Spontaneity is your middle name, and you're always up for a random adventure

9. You could give Capricorns a run for their money when it comes to determination

10. You will always defend those who cannot defend themselves

---

"I tend to have repeated arguments with my boyfriend of the past 4 years. He says he sees my habits and I know he's just trying to bring me to be more aware and do better. But most of the time it never changes and I'm doing the same negative habit. It's starting to take a toll on him and I don't want our relationship to suffer from it. What can I do to help make a change for the better and not be so forgetful about things that are important for him and our relationship?" —*Amanda*

Getting locked into the same old routine with a lover is such an easy trap to fall into, but the great news is that it's also really easy to change it. You have an awareness of what you're doing, which is fantastic, so now that you have that awareness, it's time to do something with it. These repeated arguments with your boyfriend are like a dance that you both know the steps to. After four years, you probably know exactly how each argument is going to go. But here's the thing with a dance: if one partner changes the steps, the other partner is forced to change their steps too. Next time the same old argument threatens to rear its ugly head, do something different. Start dancing. Kiss your man. Ask him if he wants to go for a walk with you. Tell him what you love about him. Don't take the bait: change the dance!

The second piece to this is the key to all relationships. Instead of focussing on what your lover is doing that you don't like, start to obsess about how much you love your life. Get high on feeling good, and then turn your focus to him, and all the ways you love and appreciate him. When you feel great, you will draw him into feeling great too. Crowd out the negativity by overdosing on what is good. This will absolutely transform your relationship. I can't wait for you to try it out. ♥

APRIL

"A WOMAN IS POWERFUL WHEN HER FIRST WORD ISN'T 'SORRY'. A WOMAN IS POWERFUL WHEN YOU FORGET WHO THE MAN IN HER LIFE IS. A WOMAN IS POWERFUL WHEN SHE FOLLOWS HER GUT. ANY WOMAN WHO BELONGS TO HERSELF HAS POWER, AND THAT POWER IS PERCEIVED AS DANGEROUS." —JOAN JULIET BUCK

ACTIVITY SHEET

THIS MONTH, I WILL EXPERIENCE A REBIRTH OF MY SOUL.

I will leave the following bad habits in the dust:

_____
_____
_____
_____

I will replace them with the following:

_____
_____
_____
_____

When I feel like I am about to fall back into an old mode of being, I will:

_____
_____
_____
_____

I will support myself in this change by:

_____
_____
_____
_____

When I make these changes, I will feel:

_____
_____
_____
_____

...And that is worth all the discomfort in the universe!

20
Spring things

THINGS TO DO IN SPRING

SPRING LIST

1. Put a mirror ball in the sunniest corner of your home
2. Hang a neon sign above your bed
3. Invest in bamboo sheets
4. Write one haiku poem every day
5. Start planning a summer vacation
6. Take a class that fascinates you
7. Watch a documentary about your favourite pop star
8. Turn up the music until it floods your entire house and gives you goosebumps all over
9. Make a wish every morning
10. Fill your home with plants
11. Burn anything your ex ever gave you (see also: Love Rehab)
12. Add drops of sweet orange oil to a diffuser and let your room fill with the scent
13. Get a spray tan before you really need one (it will make you feel good)
14. Listen to Abraham Hicks videos when you're getting ready in the mornings
15. Have a picnic in your bedroom with your favourite person
16. Venture into the city and investigate some cool art or museums
17. Claim Rihanna as your official bad girl icon
18. Change your signature so that it is way more fabulous
19. Invest in massage or acupuncture
20. Give a copy of your favourite book to a person you'd like to know better

ADVICE

"How long did it take you to heal yourself and find someone new after divorce? I'm feeling very blah after my marriage fell apart and looking forward to the excitement of a new romance but don't know how long I should wait before I get back out there."
—*Emily*

Here's an essential rule of life: don't compare your life to anyone else's, including mine. My divorce was a blessing, and as soon as my husband moved out, I breathed an enormous sigh of relief. I walked into my newly empty apartment, heard the door click behind me, and felt a huge wave of peace wash over me. I was free! I went on to have the most wonderful summer ever, with no one to answer to but myself. Not everyone feels this way when their marriage ends… But a lot of people do.

If you're feeling blah, honor your feelings. It's okay to feel that way, but make sure you're not staying in that emotional place just because it's comfortable to feel bad. Make feeling good your priority, and do whatever it takes to get there.

To answer your question: I met my boo after only a couple of months, and it happened so quickly that I thought it was a fluke. I even asked my friend Ophira about it, and she said, "It's not a fluke. You're so clear on what you want—because you've been experiencing what you don't want for so long—that of course he showed up almost immediately."

#truethat.

Here are a few others things that helped our love manifest:

- I was SO psyched on life when I met him. Everything was amazing. I was going out dancing with my friends a lot, I had just sold my first book to Hay House, and I was reading in bed, listening to stand-up comedy all the time, writing, dressing up, travelling the world, and absolutely living my best life. Think back on all the times you've created great things: you were rocking a really rad vibe. Your vibe is everything, and a high one attracts the best people. This is not a coincidence.

- I wasn't looking for love, or even a boyfriend. In fact, I only started dating because my friend Rabbit told me I should, and I was doing it more out of curiosity than anything. (I love meeting new people.) I was already casually seeing a guy who made me laugh when I met my now beloved, and I was so "whatever" about it that I was totally dressed down on our first date. Thankfully, our chemistry was undeniable! But the major point here is that I was absolutely complete on my own, and had no need for a dude to make my life special. It was already full to the brim.

- I had written a list of what I wanted in my next relationship, which did not, by the way, include any physical attributes. It was all about how we FELT together. And then—major key—I tucked it into a drawer and promptly forgot about it. This is essentially Ordering From The Universe 101. I didn't even remember I'd written it until I stumbled on it a few months later and realised that my new relationship ticked every single box!

- Falling in love is wonderful, but it's not everything. The goal should always be to build yourself up, create your own world, and fill your life with so much joy that a partner is just a drizzle of caramel on the top of your ice cream sundae. It will all happen in perfect timing, I promise. ❤

10 REASONS WHY IT'S GREAT TO BE A

Taurus

1. Know how to soak up life

2. You move at your own pace

3. Deliciously in the present moment

4. You never skimp on the things that will make you feel good

5. People always feel comfortable in your home

6. You're loyal until the very end

7. You always see the best in others and love them for their potential

8. You're such a romantic, even when you're not trying

9. So generous—you will give and give without expecting anything in return

10. You love to experiment in bed and soak up all things sensual

MAY

"I HOPE EVERYONE COULD GET RICH AND FAMOUS AND HAVE EVERYTHING THEY EVER DREAMED OF, SO THEY WILL KNOW IT'S NOT THE ANSWER." —JIM CARREY

ACTIVITY SHEET

THIS MONTH, I WILL SHOW MY LOVE TO OTHERS RELENTLESSLY.

Here are three little things I can do to show love:

Here are three big things I can do to show love:

When I'm feeling tired or small, I will remember the times that people showed me love by:

…And I will recall how important that was, and how it renewed my spirit.

I will show my love to others because:

FIVE PARTY IDEAS

THROW THESE PARTIES DURING THE YEAR

Any occasion is a good occasion to throw a fabulous party! You don't need to wait until your birthday or the holidays to break out decorations, send invitations, or fill your bathtub with bottles of champagne! Why, you could do that every weekend if you felt the call.

I was so inspired by RuPaul's response when an interviewer asked him what his plans were in this new political climate. He essentially said he was going to party like it was 1999! In the face of so much horror, it is our responsibility to step our pussies up! It is our responsibility to become even more raucous, colourful, bright, bold, and lascivious. And that's an invitation I absolutely cannot resist.

Here are five easy party ideas that will—I can almost guarantee—result in the most fun night ever!

1. PINK PARTY

If you love pink like I do, this one is such a no-brainer. Wear pink from head to toe, serve rosé and pink lemonade, replace your regular lightbulbs with pink ones, give out tiny bowls of strawberry ice-cream, hang a neon sign so your living room glows (you can buy great, inexpensive ones on Amazon!), have an assortment of pink lipsticks and a big sheet of paper on the wall which you encourage guests to kiss, paint each others' nails, hang portraits of Angelyne, and snap photos with a piece of clear pink film taped over the lens! It will be so dreamy. Send me pictures!

2. WIG PARTY

Wigs are the most fun thing ever. I recently started to amass a collection and I now have at least six, all of which I am obsessed with. The best part is that whenever I tell people about them, they get so excited and want to come over and try them all on! So why not turn that into an event?! Have each guest bring at least one wig with them for try-on and swapping purposes. I find the best ones on Amazon: the trick is to read the reviews! Put on some of your favourite tunes, pop a bottle, and enjoy the thrill of experimenting with your hair.

3. POEM PARTY

Slide the invitations inside old poetry books and give them out to intended guests. Write your favourite poems, sonnets and haikus on huge pieces of paper, then hang them all over your house. Come up with custom cocktails named after your favourite poets. Set up a typewriter with some loose paper and encourage your guests to write mini poems as the night goes on. Have everyone bring a copy of their favourite poem and do a recital! Light candles for your favourite writers. Yesssssssss.

4. GODDESS PARTY

I must confess that this one is not my original idea. It's actually an idea my friend Evelyn had, and one that she executed with a lot of style and grace last August. I wore a mostly see-through rose gold dress, there were two Aphrodites (one of whom was completely naked with the exception of a long blonde wig), and my best friend, boyfriend and I spent plenty of time lying on the floor as various goddesses hand-fed us grapes.

5. ART PARTY

Parties don't need to be held in your home or even in a traditional venue to be extra-fun. Why not gather a group of your favourite people and head to a gallery to see some works that you're really excited about? If James Turrell or Yayoi Kusama are exhibiting in a city near you, please trust me and GO! Get dressed up, take your cameras, have someone pack mini-sandwiches, and let your minds become boggled by beauty. ♥

ADVICE

"I'm in the military and have a year left in my contract. I want to get out and pursue my dreams of being a wildlife biologist, and eventually wanting to start a camp for girls who love the outdoors and adventures. But the military is job security and everybody says I should stay in. Should I? Or should I just risk it?" —*Holly*

You already know what you want to do, you're just looking for permission! You want to bust out of there! To me, it all depends on how much you love or hate your job. If it's not terrible, I'd stay, stack that paper, and organise everything, so that when you go to school next year, you have money to live on and you can devote yourself fully to your studies. I love your idea of starting a camp for outdoorsy girls! Maybe you can even start doing weekend getaways while you're in school—bring your dream into the present, rather than keeping it in the distant future! When you start taking right actions, everything comes together. You never know whose attention you might attract, or what might fall into your lap as a result of being in the right place at the right time! Good luck! ♥

10 REASONS WHY IT'S GREAT TO BE A
Gemini

1. Brilliant, creative mind

2. Wholeheartedly throw yourself into your passions

3. Can pluck the perfect word out of the air

4. Can get along with anybody

5. You are constantly expressing yourself through your style, writing, speech, facial expressions, and more

6. Full of joy, you laugh all the time

7. You don't hold grudges—instead, you just get on with the next thing

8. You're masters and mistresses of reinvention and never get stuck in one place for long

9. Your mind is lightning-quick and you learn fast

10. You're always able to see both sides of an issue

"RECLAIM YOUR MIND AND GET IT OUT OF THE HANDS OF THE CULTURAL ENGINEERS WHO WANT TO TURN YOU INTO A HALF-BAKED MORON CONSUMING ALL THIS TRASH THAT'S BEING MANUFACTURED OUT OF THE BONES OF A DYING WORLD." —TERENCE MCKENNA

ACTIVITY SHEET

MY BIGGEST CREATIVE DREAM LOOKS LIKE:

_____
_____
_____
_____

Even though it makes me feel a bit nervous, mostly when I think about it, I feel:

_____
_____
_____
_____
_____

I know that in order to make my dreams come true, I need to step my game up.
If I was the best in the world, how would I do things differently?

_____
_____
_____
_____
_____

ACTIVITY SHEET

These are people I can reach out to
(or research) if I am feeling stuck:

_____

_____

_____

_____

_____

The very first thing
I need to do is:

_____

_____

_____

_____

The next thing to tackle is: I will complete the first task by:

_____   _____

_____   _____

Sign in blood here. Wink wink.

_____

HOW TO BE YOUR OWN STYLE ICON

If personal style intimidates you, let's change that! Think of it in the same way you think of anything else you love and have an aptitude for: you don't take it too seriously, you enjoy the process, and you play a lot. It's exactly those steps that help you figure things out! It's time to do the same thing with your own aesthetic. Sounds fun, right?!

There has never been a better time to experiment with your own style. With an internet connection, you have access to absolutely everything in the entire world. If you want to dress like a lycra-clad bondage superhero one day and a folk singer the next, you can! We have so much freedom now, and the only limit is your imagination. So let's dream really big, and let's go for it!

The way I see it, getting dressed up is an artform. It's not just about combining texture, colour, and proportion: it is also about self-expression. When I get dressed, I am telling a story! I'm portraying a mood. Sometimes I'm dressed like a schoolgirl who fights crime, other days I'm swanning around in a kimono and a turban like an eccentric heiress. You don't have to be the same person every single day. There is so much joy in showcasing the different parts of your personality... And flashing a huge smile at people who don't understand!

I have gone through so many phases (goth! Vintage! The list goes on!), and the place that I find the most pleasure is outside of a label. They are too limiting. In fact, after many years of it, I even got sick of having pink hair because it felt like it boxed me in too much. These days, I have raven black hair with pink tips... And a vast wig collection! I encourage you to switch things up on a daily basis. Surprise yourself. Make it so your lover never really knows which babe they're coming home to tonight. (That's hot.)

WANT SOME INSPIRATION AND IDEAS TO GET STARTED?

Every babe should own at least one devastatingly fabulous faux fur coat. (Pink? Lime green? Multi-coloured? You be the judge.) How would the street react if you shimmied down it in a pair of sequin flares? Maybe it's time to try out some vinyl pants (worn with devastating heels). A great synthetic wig can completely change your look for the better. You definitely need a rhinestone choker to add a bit of sparkle to the most minimal of outfits. Try a different lipstick than usual and see how it's like turning on the lights on your face! Seamless thongs (I like simple black ones by On Gossamer) are essential for line-free looks. Try a fistful of rings... Or no jewellery at all. Wear stilettos with athleisure. Hunt down a perfect pair of sunglasses. And above all... Have fun with it. ❤

ADVICE

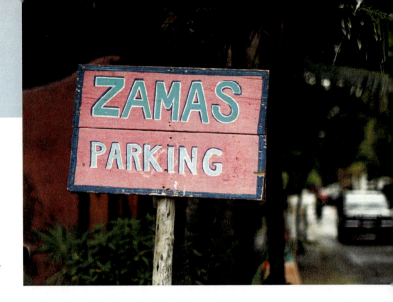

"How do you stop overthinking and being paranoid?"—*Candis*

The only thing you need to know is that your thoughts are a choice. A while ago, I realised that my mind was like a room full of trampolines, stretching out into infinity. Each thought I've ever had was represented by a trampoline, and my consciousness—the captain of the ship—was like a joyful five year old, bouncing from one trampoline to the next. In other words, we *control* how long we stay on one trampoline (or one thought). If the thought we are thinking doesn't make us feel good, *we have the power to change the thought.* We can go in a different direction. We can think something else. We can hop from that trampoline to an entirely new one.

We don't have to torture ourselves with our own thoughts. IT IS OPTIONAL.

That is one of the biggest lessons I learned in 2017. The last week of November, I felt like I popped through a wormhole and looked back at the year in amazement. I realised that the reason it had felt like I'd had a shitty year was because I had been administering capital punishment in my mind!

I was obsessing over things I couldn't control.
I was always wishing things were different.
I was frustrated that people wouldn't do what I wanted them to do.
I was fixated on the litany of things that I *didn't* want to happen.

And guess what? Almost all of those things that I didn't want to happen... happened. And I CREATED THAT with my own mind!

Because I was too arrogant to count my blessings.
Because I was too stubborn to realise that the only person I can control is me.
Because I was so fearful of anything uncertain.
And because—crucially—I didn't realise the immense power of my own mind.

Even Drake sings, "The power of the mind is not a joke!" The man knows what he's talking about.

So: how do you stop overthinking?

Cultivate a Sacred Morning practice. Become aware of your thoughts and when you notice that they don't feel good, think *something* else! Make a gratitude list in your mind. Call a friend. Read a book. Have an orgasm (although, maybe not in the workplace. But then, maybe so! No judgment!). Remember that you are in charge of your mind, and that you are not your thoughts. You don't have to jump onto them and let them sail you down the river to Miserytown. Fuck that. ♥

10 REASONS WHY IT'S GREAT TO BE A

Cancer

1. You will always make the effort to make other people comfortable

2. You love to talk about emotions and feelings and process them

3. You are the definition of loving and nurturing

4. Domestic goddesses look to you for advice

5. You're sentimental and remind people of their happiest memories

6. You will give freely without expecting anything in return

7. You love getting people together and throw the best parties

8. The people in your life feel so loved by you

9. You're so patient you deserve several medals

10. You're always connected to your emotions and you know exactly how you feel

JULY

"TO WIN AT LIFE, YOU HAVE TO BE WILLING TO DIE A THOUSAND DEATHS AND BE REBORN A THOUSAND TIMES." —RUPAUL

ACTIVITY SHEET

THIS MONTH, I WILL NURTURE MY FRIENDSHIPS BY:

_____
_____
_____
_____

I will make an effort to connect with:

_____   _____
_____   _____
_____   _____

Here are some ideas I have for fun friend dates!

_____
_____
_____

☐ I pledge to return text messages   ☐ I pledge to make our interactions joyful and positive   ☐ I pledge to initiate hang-outs

Hello, beautiful. It's July!

I wanted to take this opportunity to pop in and help you do a little assessment of where you're at.

I often find that between January and July my priorities shift pretty significantly. In the midst of the hot, sticky heat of a New York summer, the things I planned to do way back in January can feel very distant—almost like someone else came up with them. Do I really want to take on this project... Or would I rather hunt out rooftop swimming pools? (Probably the latter.)

Today we're going to do an appraisal of the goals you set way back in January, and perhaps most importantly, we're going to see how you feel about them. Because that is the most important thing.

In the columns below, I'd like you to write down the major goals you had for the year, as well as the dominant emotion that comes up for you when you think about it. Don't overthink this: go with your first instinct. Okay, ready? Go! ♥

MID-YEAR CHECK-IN

GOAL

HOW I FEEL ABOUT IT

Here's how we decode this.

If the emotion you wrote down on the right-hand side is a positive one, great! Feel free to proceed with that goal and slay it like Buffy! But if it's not so positive, we need to do some further assessment.

Sometimes our feelings aren't as straight-forward as they seem. For example, while you might have written "Booooooooring" alongside one of your goals, there is a possibility that there's more lurking underneath. Maybe your reflex to denounce something as boring is really about fear. Or procrastination. Or a feeling that it won't work anyway, so why bother.

If you have an inkling that that might be what's going with some of your reactions, take some time this week to meditate on each one. This doesn't necessarily mean you need to sit cross-legged and ohm it out; you could just as easily take a long walk, think about the goal, and see what comes up.

However, if your goal is leaving you feeling genuinely uninspired, or it has shifted or become bigger, that's great! You can cross it off and make new plans.

I want to encourage you to do this this week. Clearing up the psychic energy around your goals and ambitions feels really good, it's like feng shui but for your brain. Once you are able to get a few items off your plate—as well as recommit to the ones that are still really exciting—you will have so much more energy! ♥

THINGS TO DO IN SUMMER

SUMMER LIST

1. Use Amazing Maui Babe Browning Lotion every single day
2. Lie on the beach and stare at the stars
3. Read bell hooks
4. Don't wear underwear
5. Swim naked
6. Say out loud what you're grateful for every day
7. Buy postcards
8. Go out dancing until you sweat through your clothes
9. Seek out a sound healing session
10. Get your tarot cards read
11. Buy new sex toys
12. Embrace your sensuality
13. Wear the smallest pieces of clothing you can find
14. Have outdoor dinner parties
15. Go glamping with your best friends
16. Take a pole-dancing class
17. Rock a neon mani/pedi all season long
18. Fill your house with pink roses
19. Meditate on the grass
20. Take Instax photos of absolutely everything!

ADVICE

"This month I had a birthday and I arranged to get some friends together for drinking and dancing. On the day of the celebration, people started pulling out. Two of these friends I've known 20 years. How would you respond to this situation? I feel so disappointed by these friends and hurt. I've since bounced back but I really question these friendships."—*Regine*

Your disappointment is totally understandable, especially given the fact that it was your birthday. But maybe there is a way of framing this up so that it isn't disappointing. Maybe there is a way of framing this so that your friends have actually, without meaning to, given you a gift. And I think they have. They have given you the gift of clarity and truth.

Now, those are prickly gifts to receive: like someone handing you a bouquet of thorny roses. It might hurt when you accept the gift, but once you trim the stems and put the roses in a vase, they are beautiful and life-enhancing, and you can almost forget the thorns.

So it is with them. They have shown you, by their actions, who they really are. They have demonstrated their apathy, their resistance to joy, their selfishness. And now you get to decide what you will do with this gift.

I have found, over the years, that the best thing to do with truth is to look it square in the eye and then take a big gulp of it. The alternative—to pretend everything is fine and look the other way—always leads to regret and a mess.

You don't need these people in your life if they are only adding pain and disappointment. You deserve to spend time with people who make you feel precious and special every single time you hang out. The good news is that as you become more aware of this fact, your vibration will change, and you will begin to attract people who do exactly that. They are just around the corner. It's all going to be wonderful. ♥

10 REASONS WHY IT'S GREAT TO BE A

Leo

1. Truly, you have great hair

2. Everyone feels you when you walk into a room

3. Your energy is totally regal and radiant

4. In your heart, you know your inherent worth

5. You love to bring the drama and you know how to put on a show

6. You don't believe there's such a thing as being overdressed

7. You're relentlessly fun-loving

8. Self-expression is everything

9. You're at your most wonderful when you're the centre of attention

10. When you love someone, you love them with your entire heart

"IF SOMEONE REALLY WANTS TO HURT YOU, THEY'LL FIND A WAY WHATEVER. I DON'T WANT TO LIVE MY LIFE WORRYING ABOUT IT." —GEORGE MICHAEL

ACTIVITY SHEET

THREE ESSENTIAL ITEMS IN MY RADICAL SELF LOVE TOOLKIT:

Three things that help when
I'm feeling anxious or panicked:

Three songs that make me feel great
every single time I hear them:

Three movies that I can
quote endlessly:

Three affirmations that
feel true and beautiful:

Thoughts to COOL You Down

- An Ice cube down your back
- A hole in your shoe when it's raining
- Pressing yourself against a tile wall
- Running through the spray of a waterfall
- Dancing a jig on an iceberg with a Polar Bear

- Becoming a snowflake

- The inside of an abandoned typewriter
- Popping the emergency exit on a plane and being sucked out of the aircraft
- Floating in space naked

- Being sprayed with liquid nitrogen and immediately freezing in place

- Worm Holes

Love,
GALA

ADVICE

"What's your advice for not letting an extremely toxic coworker absorb your energy?"—*Aileen*

Maintaining our energy is one of the most vital things we can do, and yet it is something we are never taught. It's wild, because when we feel drained of energy or just low in energy, it affects everything around us. We cannot be our most vivacious selves because… we're tired. We just want to go back to bed. And that is such a bummer! I don't want to move through the world half-asleep, do you?

Approximately a million years ago (read: 2006, but it feels like another lifetime), I made friends with an English man wearing a cowboy hat. We were at Burning Man, it was very dusty, I was wearing faux fur legwarmers, and he was teaching a mini workshop on how to access your psychic ability. It was very fortuitous, because just half an hour beforehand, I had been telling a friend about how I wanted to learn more about psychic powers.

Anyway, this man—his name is Ed—and I became friends, and in addition to teaching me about how to tune into my intuition, he also taught me about protecting my energy. It turns out that when we don't make an effort to safeguard our energy, it gets battered about: by other people, by the environment, by stress. So it is our job to make sure it is looked after.

There are two easy ways to do this, both of which I a) do regularly and b) recommend thoroughly.

The first is called the Disco Ball technique, and you do it before you leave your house in the morning. It's so quick! All you do is visualise yourself inside—you guessed it—a disco ball! The idea of the disco ball is that it protects your energy by keeping all your good vibes sealed inside it, and deflects anything nasty that anyone else might direct towards you. With a disco ball, only their positivity will come through to your energetic field!

The second technique is called Zipping Up. I like to layer this in when I feel the need, although I must admit I feel the need to do this less and less these days as I have more control over my own energy. Essentially it's great as an added layer of protection. You simply imagine a big zipper that starts at your pubic bone, and envision zipping it all the way up your body and over your head. This big zipper contains your energy and, weirdly enough, kind of makes you invisible to people whose attention you don't want. I love to use this technique when passing groups of men on the street. It really changes their behaviour. They still look, but they don't say shit! And that's how I like it! ♥

10 REASONS WHY IT'S GREAT TO BE A

Virgo

1. You have the gift of total discernment

2. You'll outwork your competition every single time (see also: Beyonce and Michael Jackson)

3. You never miss a detail (you'll always fix your friend's bangs and typos)

4. Half-assing something is never an option

5. You are always up on the latest information, news, trends

6. You believe in the power of personal style and being well-dressed

7. You love to give, to help others, to show up and support the people in your life

8. You're a chameleon and can fit in anywhere

9. You always remember small things people mention which makes you an amazing gift-giver

10. You MEAN what you SAY!

SEPTEMBER

"LIFE IS A CONSPIRACY TO SHOWER YOU WITH A NONSTOP FEAST OF INTERESTING EXPERIENCES, ALL OF WHICH ARE DESIGNED TO HELP YOU GROW YOUR INTELLIGENCE, SHED YOUR PRETENSIONS, AND MASTER THE ART OF INGENIOUS LOVE." —ROB BREZSNY

ACTIVITY SHEET

THIS MONTH, I WILL ACCEPT AND ADORE MYSELF AS I AM, BECAUSE I AM RAD AS FUCK. MY 13 YEAR OLD SELF WOULD BE IN AWE!

Here is just a sampling of the badass things I have done over the last ten years:

_____
_____
_____
_____
_____
_____

Here are just a few of the things I love about myself:

_____
_____
_____
_____
_____

Here are just a few of the amazing things I am going to do in the future:

_____
_____
_____
_____
_____

STOP THE J WORD

Jealousy

FROM KILLING GIRL LOVE

I first read the title of this piece in one of Bikini Kill's original riot grrrl zines. I never owned the real thing, of course—living in New Zealand meant that I missed out on so many amazing pieces of 90s culture. But I did have the internet, and my obsessive searches led me to the most incredible things, riot grrrl being one of them.

Riot grrrl was a movement that started in the early 90s in the Northwest of the USA. Young women within the punk rock scene started getting pissed off by being pushed to the back of the room, so they began to form their own bands, have shows where women were invited to the front of the pit, and spread their ideologies within zines (handmade magazines). These zines were typically typewritten, xeroxed, and mailed all over the country.

I always think of Kathleen Hanna—lead singer and founding member of Bikini Kill—as the queen of the riot grrrls, and Bikini Kill's zines were super-influential in my own life. In both their zines and their songs, they talked about anger, about the pressures of being female, and also about the importance of women coming together to overcome the struggles that are thrown our way.

There are so many pieces that need to come together in order for us to truly own our lives and have complete autonomy, and one of the biggest parts is in refusing to be threatened by or made insecure by other women.

I have to admit, this isn't always easy. In fact, for years I was threatened by other women. Were they prettier, smarter, wealthier, more charming? If I didn't feel like I measured up in one of those categories, we had a problem… And if I felt like they were doing better than me in more than one way, then *watch out*. The shit—at least in my mind—would really hit the fan. It's a horrible way to feel, to feel unworthy in your own skin, all because some other woman *simply exists*.

Something happened last time I was in Tulum that completely changed how I viewed other women. I was with one of my best friends, Veronica Varlow. We had just come from a three-hour meditation ceremony in a treehouse and we were feeling truly blissed out. We had walked back to our hotel along the beach, with a blazing moon casting enormous shadows on the sand, and a lightning storm flickering in a distant cloud. It was late at night, so we walked into our hotel's restaurant, desperately hoping they might have some food on offer. As we walked in, we ran into Eli, a man we had met earlier that day. Eli was in his 60s and ran a lot of the wellness activities in Tulum—definitely a good person to know.

"Eli!", we cried. "We're so hungry!"

Eli beamed at us and led us over to his table, which was populated by a huge group of people.

"Come over here," he said. "We're just finishing up, but there might be something for you to eat."

I noticed a beautiful blonde woman sitting at the end of the table with her friends, but as we approached—as if

in slow motion—I watched her turn her head towards us with the most disdainful look I've ever seen. In that very instant, I knew and understood exactly what the look meant. I had made that face so many times, and I had felt the way she felt when I had been faced with a woman that I thought was somehow better than I was.

I grabbed Veronica's arm and turned her sideways, away from the table.

"Oh my god," I said. "Did you see that woman's face?"

Veronica turned to look, and then turned back to me.

"Wow," she said.

"Do you know how many times I have felt that way?" I asked her. "For so many years, I have been in a constant state of THAT FACE. This is such a huge wake-up call for me. It is a lesson. I can see now how insane it is. There is nothing to be threatened by, ever. That woman is beautiful and we don't want anything from her. There is nothing to fear."

The lesson kept being repeated over the next few days, because it seemed like no matter where we went, this woman would show up. As we were sitting outside eating tacos, she'd trek past us in the sand, averting her eyes. It must have driven her crazy. The final time we saw her was at one of my favourite spots in Tulum, Raw Love, an outdoor cafe. Veronica and I were standing at the counter ordering smoothies when I turned slightly and saw her

The most important thing in life is that we make feeling good our #1 priority.

---

sitting at a table opposite us. She was sitting with her man, and she was literally covering the side of her face with her hand so she wouldn't have to see us. I couldn't believe what a visceral response she was having.

I honestly believe that those encounters over the course of a few days cured me of the insecurity I had been feeling for, well, as long as I could remember. It was so shocking to me, because this woman was gorgeous, with a loving family, lots of friends, and she was in one of the dreamiest places on earth… But her peace of mind was destroyed by something as simple as Veronica and I walking past.

Then I realised: she and I are no different, just like you and I are no different. We are so unique and wonderful in our own ways, there is never any need for comparison. And even when you ask yourself a ridiculous question such as, 'Is this person better than me?', you'll realise there is no real answer. People simply cannot be compared and you will never know the full story of what someone else is doing or experiencing anyway. People who seem deliriously happy can be struggling with the most incredible challenges.

The most important thing in life is that we make feeling good our #1 priority. It's easy to get thrown off the scent of feeling good when something like insecurity or jealousy rears its ugly head, but it's equally easy to get back on track. All we have to do is PRACTICE GRATITUDE and it will bring us back to equilibrium.

If you're feeling bad about yourself, or sorry for yourself, or angry about something that someone has done… Take a deep breath. Remember that being in this place is a *choice*, and you can choose to feel good right now. And it's such a no-brainer, isn't it? Feeling good always feels better than feeling bad! You can move out of this bad mood by stepping back and taking a moment to express gratitude. Think about what you love about yourself, or your partner. Let your mind meander over all the things in your life that you are so, so, deeply thankful to have.

I was speaking a gratitude list aloud to one of my friends the other day, and when I got done talking about everything that I was thankful for, I gasped. I had forgotten the number one thing, which was that I was so thankful that I love myself, that I can rely on myself, that I have never abandoned myself, that I keep on going. As long as I have that, I have everything I need… And you do too.

Projecting onto someone else because of our own insecurities never feels good. If you changed your attitude about it, those girls that you envy or feel jealous of could be your best friends! Imagine how much fun you could have together! Imagine what you could learn from one another, imagine how you could uplift and inspire each others!

Replace insecurity with appreciation, and you will transform your life. ♥

ADVICE

"I want to ask you for some tips for keeping it fresh and exciting in the bedroom. Me and my man are open about it but I feel like I'm not as confident as I can be because of some issues we've had. You're a big idol of mine and always open to hearing new methods to feeling confident!" —*Kaite*

This is such a great question because it is something that we all rub up against (haha) at one stage or another. Love is incredible and sex is wonderful but after a while, you want to mix it up. This is the entire subject of my forthcoming book, and I cannot wait to share it with you! But here is my short answer to your question.

The two best things you can do for your sex life—both alone and with others!—is to work on BEING PRESENT and BEING CONFIDENT. As you can probably imagine, these are pieces of the puzzle that fit together, that flow back and forth, that inform one another. It is rare that someone would be confident in the bedroom but also be in her head all the time, just as it is unlikely that you'd be fully in your body but lack confidence. These two facets work in tandem.

Being present in bed is about feeling good. It is about alignment! That is what sensuality really is: it is about being fully aligned with yourself, and then using that good energy to move about, to express yourself, to turn sex into a dance or a place where you can play. Being present is the *opposite* of thinking about your to-do list.

Being confident in bed is about being fully embodied and not worrying about what you look like. It's about feeling free enough to do what you really want to do, being able to look your lover in the eye and show them what you like, feeling safe enough within yourself that you move decisively but fluidly.

If you work on these two skills, your sex life will automatically get better. There are so many ways you can work on these things, most of them esoteric. Don't you just love that?! You can tap on it (galadarling.com/tapthat), you can listen to binaural beats (they're on Youtube!), you can do guided meditations, you can chant, you can visualise, you can exercise, you can use a yoni egg, you can work sex magic, and the list goes on. If you are holding onto trauma, see a healer. Get acupuncture. Dance. Get regular massages. Do whatever you feel you need to do to get into your own body.

All of these techniques will help bring you closer to yourself, to your true essence, to your unique sensuality... And then your sex life can't help but be explosively delightful. ❤

10 REASONS WHY IT'S GREAT TO BE A

Libra

1. You're always easy to be with

2. You're interested in how things look (and want to make them look better)

3. You rate fairness and justice as being more important than almost anything

4. You thrive within partnerships

5. You're complimentary and kind: you love to lavish people with praise

6. You're never afraid to speak up for what is right

7. You're a natural leader—and not a pushy one, either

8. You have great listening skills

9. You're peaceful and always want people to be relaxed

10. You're a natural trendsetter and innovator!

OCTOBER

"THE ONE PERSON WHO WILL NEVER LEAVE US, WHOM WE WILL NEVER LOSE, IS OURSELF. LEARNING TO LOVE OUR FEMALE SELVES IS WHERE OUR SEARCH FOR LOVE MUST BEGIN." —BELL HOOKS

ACTIVITY SHEET

This month, I will embrace luxury by:

_____
_____
_____
_____

Even though sometimes it makes me feel unworthy to do nice things for myself, I will remind myself that I am:

_____
_____
_____
_____

The positive knock-on effects of embracing luxury are:

_____
_____
_____
_____

...And I am so ready for that!

Shrug off fear. 💗 Imagine what you could do if you followed every single one of your dreams. 💗 Rub essential oils into your palms to sweeten your story. 💗 Cultivate bizarre and unlikely friendships. 💗 Have dress-up parties. 💗 Commit to things with enthusiasm. 💗 Be in your body. 💗 Reach out to people you admire. 💗 Do kind things, just because. 💗 Write love letters. 💗 Spoil yourself. 💗 Stop living in your phone. 💗 Go out dancing in a pair of sequin pants. 💗 Trip out over your own fantasies. 💗 Write poems on your wall. 💗 Love unabashedly. 💗 Be generous. 💗 Delete your Facebook account. 💗 Endeavour to surprise yourself every single day. 💗 Buy fresh flowers for your bedroom. 💗 Be the person you always dreamed of meeting. 💗 Marry yourself.

20 things 0

THINGS TO DO IN FALL

FALL LIST

1. Stock your bathroom with delicious bath products
2. Buy a really fun hat that you can't wait to wear
3. Support your favourite artists and hang new pictures all over your house
4. Dress your pet in silly cozy costumes
5. Do a photobooth tour of your city
6. Take a long train ride to a place you've never visited before
7. Eat your body weight in mac and cheese
8. Have a weekly creative date with one of your best friends
9. Feng shui your entire house
10. Do a love spell and keep it under your bed
11. Get a full body massage
12. Start taking Wellness Formula vitamins (life-changing!)
13. Buy a pair of cozy sweats that you feel cute in
14. Make grand plans
15. Get eyelash extensions and wear less make-up
16. Go horse riding
17. Make holiday plans that you feel genuinely excited about
18. Forgive yourself
19. Volunteer
20. Get a tiny tattoo that no one else knows about

ADVICE

"I love the manifestation work and magic I know I'm capable of. But sometimes it's hard to stay consistently high vibe. I don't want everything to get derailed because I woke up late and don't have time for my morning ritual, and then it seems so hard to get back on track! Any advice on how to stay high vibe even when life gets a little crazy?" —Michaela

Yes, absolutely! As much as I adore the idea of using my bed as a temple and having a Sacred Morning practice, there are times when it is simply not feasible. Sometimes, I have to get up and go. Sometimes there are things that need to be tended to. This is just how life is.

This is when emotional mastery and radical self love kick in, because these are things we can practice all day long. This can be as simple as being really present on your walk to work (walking meditation!), or as seemingly complex as keeping your social circle clear of drama queens and toxicity.

Snatch little pockets of time to devote to yourself. A five minute meditation in the bathroom can be a lifesaver during a stressful morning. Taking a few moments to send a love-filled text message will make you and your recipient feel good. Remembering to focus on what you're thankful for—instead of ruminating on what's pissing you off this morning—will totally change your vibe.

As much as we might think getting into our ideal mode is about the actions we take, it is actually mostly about the thoughts we think, and we can switch those up at any time. Isn't that liberating?! I love that!

If you can keep that idea in mind, I think you'll be absolutely wonderful, no matter how late you wake up! ❤

10 REASONS WHY IT'S GREAT TO BE A

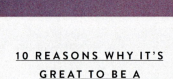

Scorpio

1. You're unafraid to get deep and be real
2. You have unabashed sex appeal
3. You're loyal until the bitter end
4. You're so mysterious that people can never forget you
5. Independent is your middle name: you don't need no (wo)mans!
6. You're passionate, spontaneous, and experimental
7. You're competitive, not just with others, but with yourself
8. You have no patience for simple or dishonest people
9. Your magnetic charm draws people in easily
10. You're intense—and the people who love you wouldn't have it any other way!

NOVEMBER

"THE WORLD IS CHANGED BY YOUR EXAMPLE,
NOT BY YOUR OPINION." —TIM FERRISS

ACTIVITY SHEET

**THIS MONTH, I WANT TO FOCUS ON BEING
THE BEST VERSION OF MYSELF I CAN BE.**

I could be kinder in the following situations:

_____
_____
_____
_____

I could be more patient with: I could spend more time with or at:

_____   _____
_____   _____
_____   _____

How would it make me feel if I did those things?

_____

I will choose one instance from each category (circle it!), and then, I will do it!

ADVICE

"Lately I've been feeling very jealous and just angry with my relationship. I realise I'm not mad at my long term boyfriend, but I just get jealous of his old relationship. He doesn't compare me or our relationship to what he used to have, but I find myself jealous and angry whenever I see his ex-girlfriend. I have no contact with her but sadly in this day and age, I see her on social media. Whether it's my own friends commenting and liking her pictures, even my boyfriend's sister is still close with her. I almost feel like I'm competing with her for my relationship?"—*Gloria*

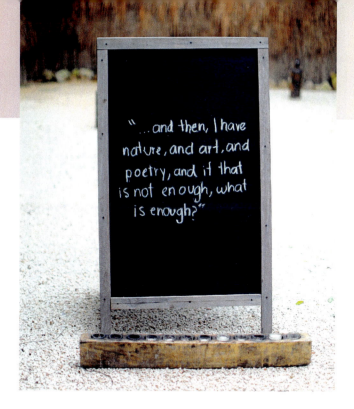

You are not competing with her for your relationship. Your boyfriend has shown no inclination that he compares the two of you, but somehow, her existence makes you uneasy. (Oh, how easy it would be if she simply got voted off the island after the break-up, right?!) Unfortunately, this is the case for almost everyone. Our lover's ex-lovers still hang around, like a bad smell, just... existing. (How dare they!) Don't they know that it is *our time now?!*

I'm messing with you because I'm trying to get you to see how silly you are being. I love you. You are great. But your focus is on *his ex* when really it should be on you and on your relationship.

The solution to a problem like this is to get so involved with your own life—and get so high on yourself!—that you don't even have time to think about things like this. Remind yourself of the myriad ways in which you are *infallibly awesome*. Bring fun back into your relationship and surprise your boyfriend with impromptu dates, movie nights, and sexy role-playing! Get back on your creativity jam. Make something that you always wished existed.

Honestly, this is the answer to almost any problem.

I promise that when you get *fully involved* in your own life, these intrusive thoughts will subside. If they ever do pop up, you'll be able to bat them away quickly, because you have so many other things going on! Make things make things make things! Fall deeply in love with yourself and the infinite possibilities of the universe! Switch your focus. Move your attention to the great things in your life, and you will watch them multiply... And your so-called "problems" will fall away, like petals in the breeze. ♥

10 REASONS WHY IT'S GREAT TO BE A

Sagittarius

1. You're always a good time, literally the life of the party

2. You have such a raunchy sense of humour, you could make anyone blush!

3. Your stores of natural optimism are a wonderful asset

4. You have an inherent love of the world around you

5. You make friends everywhere you go

6. You're honest until the end, and cannot resist telling the truth

7. Exercise and movement heals you

8. You love travelling so much that being in a foreign environment invigorates you rather than scaring you

9. Risk-taking is part of your DNA

10. You love a deep conversation, and can always get people to open up

"THERE IS ONLY ONE WAY TO HAPPINESS AND THAT IS TO CEASE WORRYING ABOUT THINGS WHICH ARE BEYOND THE POWER OR OUR WILL." —EPICTETUS

ACTIVITY SHEET

Looking back at 2018, these were my highlights:

_____
_____
_____
_____
_____
_____
_____
_____
_____
_____
_____
_____
_____
_____
_____
_____
_____
_____

ACTIVITY SHEET

But I could probably have done without:

_____
_____
_____
_____
_____
_____
_____
_____
_____
_____

That having been said, I did learn _____

and I have a new appreciation for _____

To end 2018 on a high note, I am going to focus on _____

and the first piece of that puzzle means I need to _____ Let's go!

ADVICE

"I find myself doubting my self a lot and comparing myself to others a lot which is something I really dislike. What are some ways I can stop this?" —*Angie*

Firstly, remember your inherent divinity. Know that comparison is a waste of a time and it's never the full story. Write a list of things you love about yourself. Accept yourself as you are, and acknowledge that you are perfect right now, in this moment.

But if you still find yourself comparing, make a list of the things you admire about the other person. Which of those traits could you cultivate within yourself?

You see, you are never powerless. It is never hopeless. Never over.

You are the architect of your own life. You have absolute control over it. So if you meet someone that seems to have the things that you want, you don't have to throw up your hands in defeat and feel small. No! You can be whoever you want! If you admire her social skills, practice your own! If you like the way she puts outfits together, spend a little more time experimenting with your wardrobe. If her business appears to be doing well, study why!

Jealousy and envy are really great signposts. They show us where we wish we were more, or better, or bigger. AND WE CAN BE! Do you want to be a badass warrior with buns of steel? It can be you! Do you want to run a multi-million dollar business? This is absolutely possible! Do you want to be a sex goddess who oozes confidence? You can begin today!

Nothing about who we are is as fixed as we think it is. We are pliable, flexible, bendable pieces of consciousness... And we can direct our energy and focus in absolutely any direction. This is one of the coolest things about being alive: the ability to absolutely craft our lives however we like. That is freedom!

If someone is bringing out a sense of competition or comparison in you, thank them in your mind. And then get to work becoming the person you have always wanted to be. ♥

10 REASONS WHY IT'S GREAT TO BE A

Capricorn

1. You give the best, most practical advice

2. You can solve almost all of the world's problems

3. You always know what to do next

4. You can be relied upon to do what needs to be done

5. You have the sharpest bullshit detector

6. You're insanely driven and determined: once you set your mind to something, there is no question that you will do it

7. You are stable, calm and collected in a crisis

8. You're tough! It takes a lot to make a Capricorn crumble under pressure (in fact, I've never seen that happen)

9. Your wicked sense of humor is unparalleled

10. You only get more youthful and beautiful with age!

BY THE ASTROTWINS
OPHIRA & TALI EDUT

2018 ASTROLOGY OVERVIEW

ASTROLOGY OVERVIEW

Could sweet stability be in the stars in 2018? We're cautiously optimistic, after the last few years of cosmic chaos. But a peek upstairs reveals a little more quiet than we've had in recent times. Will that echo down below? Here's hoping.

The slower-moving outer planets, which shape the larger trends that affect us all, will spend the bulk of 2018 in receptive, reflective "yin" (earth and water) signs. This could herald a calm period, but it can also make people passive at a time when action is needed.

Representing the steadying earth element, Uranus will move into Taurus, while Saturn and Pluto are both in Capricorn. The other two outer planets are in emotional water signs: Jupiter spends most of 2018 in Scorpio while Neptune is in Pisces all year.

By mid-November, three planets (Jupiter, Saturn and Neptune) will be rooted in their "home" signs—meaning they will travel through the zodiac sign that they govern—a cycle that will last until December 2019. Effusive Jupiter will be in its native Sagittarius from November 8, 2018 until December 2, 2019; staunch Saturn is anchored in Capricorn until December 2020 and watery Neptune is in Pisces until 2024.

Planets are empowered when they're stationed at home base, so if we're lucky, this could bring a more balanced energy to the world. But it's also like getting a double-strength dose of what each planet rules—the good and the bad. We'll get twice the helping of Jupiter's optimism and global focus; a dual hit of Saturn's pragmatism and rigidity; an extra round of Neptune's compassion and its unseemly secrets.

JUPITER IN SCORPIO & SAGITTARIUS: REDEFINING POWER.

In 2018, the little things matter—a lot! Big-picture Jupiter will be in micro-focused Scorpio until November 8, training our attention on the details. Themes of life and death, real estate, long-term finances, sex and power fall under Scorpio's domain. Russia, North Korea, the European Union, the United States: Changing alliances will further reshuffle the global power structures. With truth-telling Jupiter in secretive Scorpio, we can expect more leaks and shocking reveals of "classified" information. The widespread revealing of sexual misconduct and harassment has corresponded to Jupiter's visit to Scorpio.

When Jupiter returns home to Sagittarius on November 8, international issues will take the spotlight. This entrepreneurial energy will also be a boon for startups and solopreneurs, as we'll all crave more freedom. Travel, publishing and multicultural relationships will also be hot-button topics. Moving from Scorpio to Sagittarius is like changing your viewfinder from detail-focus to wide-angle. We'll emerge from the intense depths and focus on broader, more worldly topics.

WORK & MONEY IN 2018: JUPITER, SATURN, URANUS & PLUTO STEP IN.

Get ready—the economy is going to go through some serious

Economic reform could be in the stars as revolutionary Uranus enters Taurus, the sign of money and daily work, for the first time since 1942!

reforms in 2018. Several of the outer planets will travel through signs related to finance, power, corporations and shared resources, shifting the way business is conducted in some fundamental ways.

Structured Saturn and shadowy Pluto will both spend the year in patriarchal Capricorn, ruler of big business, banks, the government and hierarchy. Saturn is here until December 2020, while transformational Pluto is touring Capricorn from 2008 to 2024. As these planetary power players inch along in the same sign, we may see a rise in monopolies but also a crackdown on scandals. Saturn is the "integrity cop" of the cosmos, exposing shady business.

This year may also bring leaner times and corporate cutbacks. However, old-school Saturn in hardworking Capricorn could revive a bootstrapping work ethic. Will all of those promised manufacturing jobs return to the United States? We'll find out in 2018. The Great Depression occurred while Saturn was in Capricorn from 1929 to 1932, and here's hoping that we learn from the mistakes of yesteryear and keep our expectations—along with the stock market—grounded in reality.

Meanwhile, generous Jupiter hovers in Scorpio, the sign of joint ventures, mergers and pooled resources, until November. The sharing economy may boom, possibly out of necessity, as people look for creative ways to consolidate and cut costs. Real estate and lending is ruled by Scorpio. Housing prices could soar, making it a seller's market. But with over-the-top Jupiter, the bubble might burst—and Scorpio's influence could bring some sketchy deals back to market. From balloon mortgages to "no money down" loans, home buyers should be careful not to get in over their heads or repeat the mistakes of the 2008 crash.

Economic reform could be in the stars as revolutionary Uranus enters Taurus, the sign of money and daily work, for the first time since 1942! The side-spinning planet visits each sign for seven years, and it will be here from May 15, 2018 until April 2026. Unpredictable Uranus will shake up business as usual, revamping the way we spend, earn, save and invest. Innovation and technology will play a role—for example, we may see the rise of "cashless" businesses and the growing automation of Artificial Intelligence (AI) replacing human labor. Uranus was in Taurus during the 1850s Gold Rush and again from 1934-42, a historical era that included the Great Depression and World War II, but also the Social Security and unemployment policies that are in effect to this day.

NEPTUNE IN PISCES: ARTISTIC & SPIRITUAL RENAISSANCE.

Countering all of this money and work-driven energy, dreamy

Neptune continues floating through its home sign of Pisces from 2012 to 2026. Neptune's touch is evident in the booming wellness movement. Yoga, meditation, crystals, retreats—all things "woo" have become decidedly mainstream as Neptune nears the halfway point of its journey. (Anyone for a $14 cold-pressed, gem-infused juice brewed with activated charcoal?) Creative, compassionate Neptune champions the arts and spurs social activism. The shadow expression of Neptune is secrecy and illusion. From brewing political scandals to genocide to ISIS, this cycle has also exposed some hidden horrors in the world.

JUPITER-NEPTUNE TRINE: GLOBAL HEALING AND COMPASSION.

Could peace finally come to our world—at least, in some small way? An awakening of higher consciousness and compassion might arise this spring, when cross-cultural ambassador Jupiter unites in a harmonious trine (120-degree angle) with soul-stirring Neptune in May of 2018. The duo will both be traveling through emotional and receptive water signs (Jupiter in Scorpio and Neptune in Pisces) most of the year, opening our hearts.

The exact trine will culminate on May 25, but they'll be in close contact from May until August. This rare and unifying cycle reminds us that, while we may be "divided" by cultures and nations, we are all one. This could be a banner moment for love, with merging-minded Scorpio and starry-eyed Pisces in the mix.

NUMEROLOGY IN 2018: AN 11/2 UNIVERSAL YEAR.

Come together! After three transitional years, a unifying numerological cycle arrives. The "2" vibration inspires partnership, and this year is especially potent because it also contains the master number "11." Universal years are calculated by adding the digits of the year (in this case 2+0+1+8 = 11; 1+1 = 2). Working together, compromising and choosing high-vibe alliances will be a strong and much-needed theme. That said, 11 is a double vibration of 1, so we can expect another year of rapid-fire change and independence, even as we move toward greater cooperation.

YEAR OF THE EARTH DOG: LOYALTY RULES.

Roll over, Rooster—El Bow Wow is in the house. After a year of the fastidious Fire Cock strutting around keeping order, the Year of the Earth Dog begins. Dog energy is playful, happy and loyal.

But to whom does that loyalty belong? Dogs are pack animals who follow a strong and decisive Alpha figure. During this Chinese zodiac cycle, we must be careful not to be seduced by strength alone. Might does not make right, and the Dog Year reminds us not to be obedient followers who succumb to authority. Praise and a pat on the head feel great, but the world needs critical thinking, not blind devotion (or seduction by biscuit).

The Dog is associated with the Western sign of Libra, a lover of beauty and grace. Lavish entertaining and formal events could make a comeback and we may see a renaissance for the design industry. The best traits to emerge from these Dog days will be humble service, friendship and kindness, and we could all use a little more of that! ❤

Excerpted from The AstroTwins' 2018 Planetary Planner by Ophira & Tali Edut. Get the complete book (paperback or PDF) with horoscopes for every sign, all year long at www.astrostyle.com/2018-guide. Take 20% off with the code GALA.

JANUARY

S	M	T	W	TH	F	S
	1	2	3	4	5	6
		● Full Moon				
7	8	9	10	11	12	13
14	15	16	17	18	19	20
		○ New Moon				
21	22	23	24	25	26	27
28	29	30	31 ● Full Moon			

FEBRUARY

S	M	T	W	TH	F	S
				1	2	3
4	5	6	7	8	9	10
11	12	13	14	15 ○ New Moon	16	17
18	19	20	21	22	23	24
25	26	27	28			

MARCH

S	M	T	W	TH	F	S
				1	2	3
				● Full Moon		
4	5	6	7	8	9	10
11	12	13	14	15	16	17 ○ New Moon
18	19	20	21	22	23	24
25	26	27	28	29	30	31 ● Full Moon

APRIL

S	M	T	W	TH	F	S
1	2	3	4	5	6	7
8	9	10	11	12	13	14
15	16 ○ New Moon	17	18	19	20	21
22	23	24	25	26	27	28
29	30 ● Full Moon					

MAY

S	M	T	W	TH	F	S
		1	2	3	4	5
6	7	8	9	10	11	12
13	14	15	16	17	18	19
20	21	22 ○ New Moon	23	24	25	26
27	28	29 ● Full Moon	30	31		

JUNE

S	M	T	W	TH	F	S
					1	2
3	4	5	6	7	8	9
10	11	12	13 ○ New Moon	14	15	16
17	18	19	20	21	22	23
24	25	26	27 ● Full Moon	28	29	30

JULY

S	M	T	W	TH	F	S
1	2	3	4	5	6	7
8	9	10	11	12 ○ New Moon	13	14
15	16	17	18	19	20	21
22	23	24	25	26	27 ● Full Moon	28
29	30	31				

AUGUST

S	M	T	W	TH	F	S
			1	2	3	4
5	6	7	8	9	10	11 ○ New Moon
12	13	14	15	16	17	18
19	20	21	22	23	24	25
26 ● Full Moon	27	28	29	30	31	

SEPTEMBER

S	M	T	W	TH	F	S
						1
2	3	4	5	6	7	8
9 ○ New Moon	10	11	12	13	14	15
16	17	18	19	20	21	22
23	24 ● Full Moon	25	26	27	28	29
30						

OCTOBER

S	M	T	W	TH	F	S
	1	2	3	4	5	6
7	8	9 ○ New Moon	10	11	12	13
14	15	16	17	18	19	20
21	22	23	24 ● Full Moon	25	26	27
28	29	30	31			

NOVEMBER

S	M	T	W	TH	F	S
				1	2	3
4	5	6	7	8	9	10
			○ New Moon			
11	12	13	14	15	16	17
18	19	20	21	22	23	24
				● Full Moon		
25	26	27	28	29	30	

DECEMBER

S	M	T	W	TH	F	S
						1
2	3	4	5	6	7 ○ New Moon	8
9	10	11	12	13	14	15
16	17	18	19	20	21	22 ● Full Moon
23	24	25	26	27	28	29
30	31					

Credits

Produced by Gala Darling (@galadarling)
Art direction and graphic design by We Are Branch (@wearebranch)
Illustrations by Gabriella Rosie (@gabriellarosie)
Art and photos by Emily Faulstich (@emilyafaulstich)
Astrology by Ophira and Tali Edut (@astrotwins)

Learn more about Gala at galadarling.com

Made in the USA
San Bernardino, CA
21 January 2018